THE WAR FOR
INDEPENDENCE

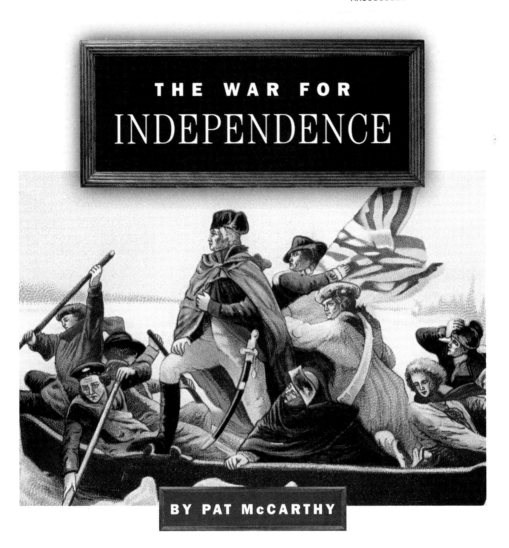

BY PAT McCARTHY

Editorial Offices: Glenview, Illinois • Parsippany, New Jersey • New York, New York

Sales Offices: Needham, Massachusetts • Duluth, Georgia • Glenview, Illinois
Coppell, Texas • Sacramento, California • Mesa, Arizona

When the American Revolution began, the colonists were not fighting for freedom from Britain. The colonists were upset about taxes made by Parliament, Britain's lawmaking body. They did not think the taxes were fair because they could not vote for members of Parliament.

Parliament passed the Stamp Act in 1765, which said the colonists had to buy stamps to put on important papers such as letters, deeds, newspapers, and playing cards. Many colonists refused to buy the stamps.

Parliament thought the taxes were fair. The French and Indian War had cost a lot of money. British soldiers had protected the colonists, so Parliament thought the colonists should help pay for the war. Parliament also passed more acts that taxed the colonists.

Events of the American Revolution

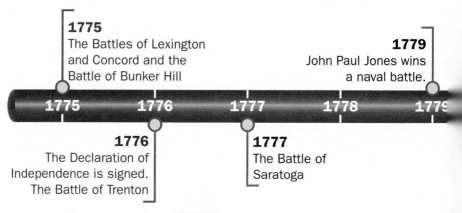

1775
The Battles of Lexington and Concord and the Battle of Bunker Hill

1779
John Paul Jones wins a naval battle.

1775 1776 1777 1778 1779

1776
The Declaration of Independence is signed.
The Battle of Trenton

1777
The Battle of Saratoga

Patriots threw British tea into Boston Harbor.

The Boston Tea Party

Parliament finally took away all the taxes but the one on tea. But the colonists were still not happy. Three ships full of tea were sent to Boston Harbor, but the people of Boston would not let them unload the tea. Britain refused to take the tea back. A group of Patriots dressed as Mohawks climbed onto the ships. They threw the tea overboard. This was known as the Boston Tea Party. No one knows who the men were, but some were probably members of a group of Patriot **activists** called the Sons of Liberty. Britain closed the port of Boston.

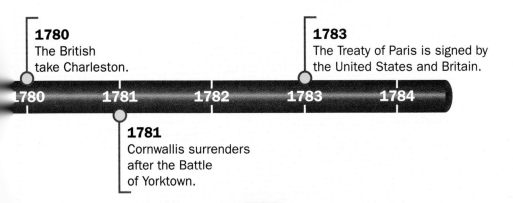

1780
The British take Charleston.

1783
The Treaty of Paris is signed by the United States and Britain.

1780   1781   1782   1783   1784

1781
Cornwallis surrenders after the Battle of Yorktown.

The Battles of Lexington and Concord

On the night of April 18, 1775, eight hundred British soldiers marched from Boston to the town of Lexington. When they reached Lexington there were about fifty soldiers waiting. They called themselves **minutemen** because they were ready to fight at a minute's notice.

The British were on their way to Concord, where the colonists stored their weapons. The night before, three horseback riders had tried to warn people that the British were coming.

The Battles of Lexington and Concord, April 1775

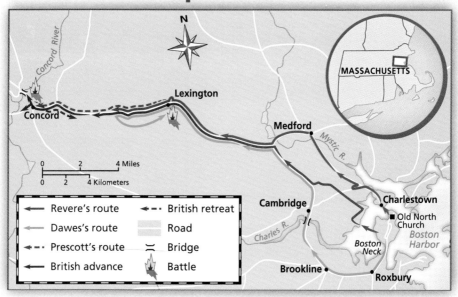

The Men Who Spread the Alarm

It was late into the night of April 18, 1775. Three men rode through the countryside in Massachusetts to warn people the British were coming. Paul Revere is the most famous of the three men, but William Dawes and Dr. Samuel Prescott did just as much.

The British captured all three men that night. Prescott escaped and made it to Concord, where he warned the people. Revere was surrounded and taken prisoner. Dawes got away as the British were capturing Revere.

In Lexington a British officer yelled, "Disperse [Move away], ye rebels, disperse!" A shot rang out. Nobody knows who fired first, but the British did not wait for orders. They began shooting. Eight minutemen were killed and ten others were wounded.

The British troops marched on to Concord and took the weapons in the storehouse. They searched houses and farms but did not find the rest of the weapons because they had been taken to other towns.

The British then returned to Boston. When the Second Continental Congress in Philadelphia heard of the battles, it chose George Washington to be in charge of the new army.

The Battle of Bunker Hill, June 17, 1775

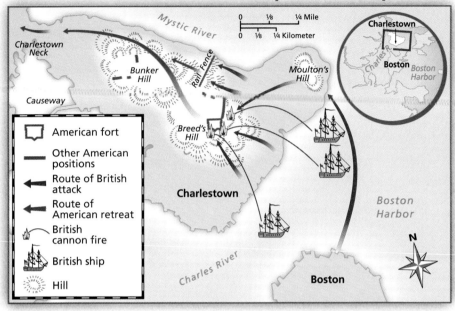

The Battle of Bunker Hill

The next major battle was the Battle of Bunker Hill. It was fought on nearby Breed's Hill. British ships were in Boston Harbor, and the Americans heard the British were going to attack.

The Americans took guns to the top of Breed's Hill during the night of June 16, 1775. They built a redoubt there. A redoubt is a fort made by piling up mounds of dirt.

When the British woke up the next morning, they were shocked to see the redoubt. They began firing from the ships, but the fort was out of range.

Two thousand British soldiers started up the hill. The Americans did not shoot until the British were close. Colonel William Prescott told his men, "Don't fire until you see the whites of their eyes."

Finally, shots rang out and dozens of British soldiers fell. Twice the British were forced to **retreat**, but the third time they were able to take the hill.

Dr. Joseph Warren was the first American officer to die in the war. He was a loyal Patriot and leader. Warren was an officer but chose to fight with his troops.

The British won the Battle of Bunker Hill, but the Americans proved they could fight well. More than one thousand British were killed or wounded. The Americans lost about 145 men.

Dr. Joseph Warren was a doctor and an American officer.

George Washington and his troops crossed the Delaware River.

During the next year and a half, several battles were fought. The Americans created a navy. France began helping the colonies. The Continental Congress wrote and signed the Declaration of Independence, which said the Thirteen Colonies were a free country.

The Battle of Trenton

On December 25, 1776, the British army was camped in Trenton, New Jersey. Most of the men were German soldiers, paid to fight for the British. Washington knew they would celebrate Christmas late into the night with dancing and singing. He decided to surprise them with an attack the next morning. During the night, 2,400 American soldiers crossed the river.

The British army was taken completely by surprise. None of Washington's soldiers were killed and only four of them were wounded. One of Washington's officers wrote in his diary, "We have taken nearly 1000 prisoners, six cannon, more than 1000 muskets, twelve drums . . . ."

Thomas Paine Gives the Army Hope

Thomas Paine

The **morale**, or spirits, of the American soldiers was low before the Battle of Trenton. The soldiers had been losing battles, were poorly trained, and had only ragged clothes.

Thomas Paine wrote the first of the *Crisis Papers*. He hoped they would keep up the morale of the Americans. On Christmas evening, Washington ordered the paper read to his troops. Many think Paine's inspiring words gave the soldiers the courage to continue fighting.

The Battle of Trenton gave the Americans supplies and weapons they needed badly. It also helped their morale. A few days later, the Americans beat the British at Princeton. In July 1777, the British took Fort Ticonderoga in New York. Marquis de Lafayette, a Frenchman, came to help and became Washington's trusted aide.

The Battle of Saratoga, 1777

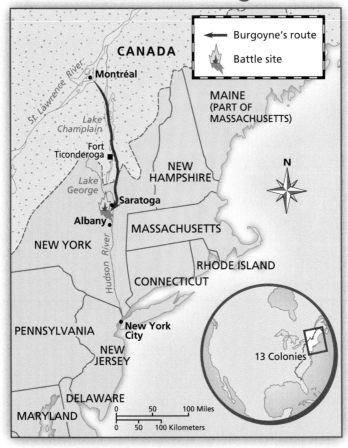

The Battle of Saratoga

British General John Burgoyne planned to send three armies into New York State. The armies would meet in Albany and cut New England off from the rest of the colonies. The Americans held the British off during the first Battle of Saratoga on September 19, 1777. General Burgoyne was forced to retreat.

Three weeks later, the Americans beat the British at Bemis Heights in the second Battle of Saratoga. This was a major American victory. Major General Horatio Gates and Major General Benedict Arnold led the American army. The two sides **negotiated** and on October 17, 1777, Burgoyne surrendered his entire army of five thousand men.

Benedict Arnold

If Benedict Arnold had died from the leg wound he got at Saratoga, he would be remembered as a great American hero. For three years, he had served the Americans as a daring military leader.

In 1780, however, he sold the British information so they could capture West

Benedict Arnold

Point. Arnold owed money and thought he should have been promoted more quickly. The plan did not work because his contact, British Major John Andre, was caught with the information Arnold had provided.

Washington led
his troops at
Valley Forge.

The Battle of Saratoga was the **turning point** of the war,
and things began to change. The world now believed the
Americans could win the war. European countries gave their
support.

In the winter of 1777, Washington's army stayed at Valley
Forge, Pennsylvania. The soldiers were cold, hungry, and often
sick. They did not have enough supplies.

In July France declared war on Britain. Now the British had
to worry about fighting two wars.

In 1779 the British asked American Indians to attack frontier
settlements. That September, the American navy, led by John
Paul Jones, fought a battle with a British ship. The British asked
him to surrender, but Jones answered, "I have not yet begun to
fight!"

The next spring the British captured Fort Moultrie in
Charleston, South Carolina. This was the worst American
defeat in the war. The Americans lost their entire Southern
Army.

British troops led by General Charles Cornwallis defeated the Americans in battles in South Carolina. Cornwallis then planned to invade North Carolina. He changed his plans after the Americans won the Battle of Kings Mountain.

General Nathanael Greene and his army chased Cornwallis through the backwoods of Virginia and the Carolinas. Cornwallis then planned to invade North Carolina. He changed his plans after the Americans won the Battle of Kings Mountain.

The Battle of Yorktown

In a brilliant move, Washington planned to attack the British on the Yorktown peninsula. French Admiral de Grasse brought ships and troops to Chesapeake Bay to help.

De Grasse's ships fought a major battle with the British ships. The British lost and retreated to New York. De Grasse kept Cornwallis from leaving the peninsula by sea.

De Grasse sent some ships up Chesapeake Bay to bring the rest of Washington's army to Yorktown. The American soldiers then started a **siege** of Yorktown. They surrounded the British, keeping them from retreating by land. British supplies ran low, and the French ships shot cannons at the British day and night.

Finally, on October 19, 1781, Cornwallis surrendered at Yorktown. This was the last major battle of the war. Britain's Parliament voted in February to stop fighting the war.

The untrained and poorly outfitted group of American Patriots had beaten the well-trained and well-supplied British army and navy. The United States of America was free at last.

Washington meets with his generals at Yorktown.

Glossary

activist a person who believes in or takes part in a cause

minutemen colonial militia groups that could be ready to fight at a minute's notice

morale the state of a person's or a group's spirits

negotiate to talk about something in order to come to an agreement

retreat to pull back a military force that is in danger from an enemy attack

siege the surrounding of an army or a town to try to make it surrender

turning point the point at which a very important change takes place